Batting

Contents

G000093455

When using this book, concentrate on one coaching point at
a time. Practise each point until you have mastered it before
moving on to the next one.
You do not need to work through the book from cover to
cover. Choose a shot you want to work on and practise it
until you are happy with the outcome.

INTRODUCTION

To win any game of cricket a team must score more runs than the opposition. That's the simple part. How you score runs, what shot you play and the way you play is all down to the individual. In international cricket there are many types of batsmen, from attacking players such as England's Kevin Pietersen to defensive ones such as India's Raul Dravid. Pietersen takes on bowlers from the start of his innings, while Dravid is known as 'the wall' because bowlers find it almost impossible to get past his defence.

This book will help you to improve your attacking shots and defence and give you top tips for facing fast bowlers or spinners. It will help you to develop a sound technique, which is essential for all top batsmen. However, every individual is different and not everyone bats in the same way. If you play your shots differently to the way described in this book and are still successful then you shouldn't change the way you bat.

WHAT MAKES A GOOD BATSMAN?

- Concentration
- Confidence
- Good shot selection
- Quick reactions and foot movement
- Ability to 'read' the game and adapt accordingly
- Patience
- Courage

PROFILE OF A BATSMAN

The best batsmen in the world have the ability to bat in different ways depending on the situation of the game. A good batsman must be able to change the way he plays depending on what his team needs him to do, the bowlers he is facing and the pitch conditions. The number a batsman bats may also affect the way he plays.

Opening batsmen must have

great courage and quick reactions to face fast bowlers with a new ball. They may be forced to play quite defensively to help the team through the difficult early stages of a match. Often the most gifted players, with the greatest array of attacking shots, bat at number 3 or 4. Batsmen at numbers 5 and 6 will have to be comfortable against both spinners and fast bowlers, and may need to be able to score runs quickly, particularly in a one-day match. Whatever their position, all batsmen need to keep concentrating over long periods of time to ensure they don't give their wicket away. Remember, it only takes one ball to get you out!

Mahendra Singh Dhoni, India's wicketkeeper-batsman, is one of the world's most exciting attacking players.

EQUIPMENT

Choosing the right equipment can be a difficult task, with so many different brands to fit a variety of budgets. Here are a few handy hints to help you choose equipment that will be comfortable and fit well.

BATS

The bat is the main tool of your trade, so choosing the right one is really important. Cricket bats are made from willow, and the quality of the bat will depend on the quality of wood used, which is reflected in the price.

The most important things to consider when buying a bat are the correct size and weight. Some parents buy children bats to 'grow into'. However, this may prevent a player developing good technique. A reasonable way to find the right bat size is to stand up straight with a bat by your side. The handle of the bat should reach the top of your thigh.

The most common mistake people make when buying a bat is to buy one that is too heavy. A good way to test if a bat is light

The bat should be light enough to pick up comfortably.

enough is to pick the bat up using your top hand only. If you are able to take a good backswing and demonstrate both straight and cross batted shots with just one hand then the bat is right for you.

PADS

Pads should always be worn when facing a hard ball. They should be big enough to cover above the knee on each leg. It is important that pads are not too big as this will cause difficulty when playing certain shots and running between the wickets. Pads should fasten so that the end of the strap is on the outside of the leg.

GLOVES

Gloves must always be worn if facing a hard ball, and there are many different styles available. Make sure your fingers fill the gloves but don't press hard against the end. It should be comfortable to fasten the gloves securely around the wrist. Gloves will have extra protection on the thumb of the bottom hand (left hand for left-handers and right for right-handers). Gloves should provide protection but also allow the hand to flex. The more gloves are worn the more they will flex.

Some batsmen like to wear inners when they bat. These are thin cotton gloves worn under batting gloves for comfort and sweat absorption. If you usually wear inners make sure that you try on gloves with inners before purchasing them.

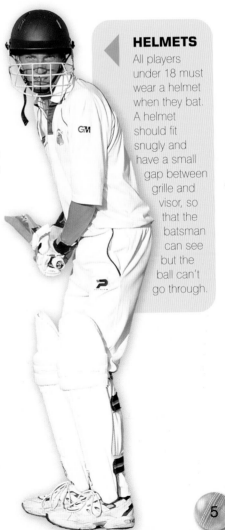

HELMETS

All players under 18 must wear a helmet when they bat. A helmet should fit snugly and have a small gap between grille and visor, so that the batsman can see but the ball can't go through.

Your grip, stance and back-lift affect every shot you play. If you get these simple things right you will avoid many common problems faced by batsmans throughout a whole range of shots.

GRIP

Practise finding your grip:

- Stand side on as if about to face a bowler and rest the bat against the inside of your front thigh. Make sure the toe of your bat is resting just behind your back foot. Leaving the bat where it is, extend both arms out to the side (see pic 1).

- Keeping your arms straight, swing both arms back towards the bat handle and clasp the bat naturally (see pic 2).

- If you are right-handed you should have your right hand at the bottom of the handle and left hand at the top (see pic 3). If left-handed, left hand at the bottom, right hand on top.

- To ensure your hands are in the right place see pic 4.

Notice how your thumb and index finger on each hand form a 'V' shape. The 'V' on each hand should be in line halfway between the spine of the bat and the outside edge. Keep your hands together in the middle of the handle.

Look over your shoulder towards the bowler, making sure you are well balanced.

STANCE

The key to a good stance is to be comfortable and balanced.

- Stand with your feet shoulder width apart, knees slightly bent. Your feet should be parallel to the batting crease, head upright and eyes level.

- Look over your front shoulder towards the bowler (see photo). You need to be balanced so you can move forward or back.

- Your shoulders and hips should point in the same direction.

- Your bat should rest behind the toes of your back foot or just in front of you, between both feet. Many batsmen tap the ground with the bat to help their concentration as they wait for the bowler.

Target

To move into position quickly and strike the ball cleanly.

BACKLIFT

As you move to play a shot, pick up the bat in a straight line. Make sure the outside edge of the bat points up so that the bat face points towards the off-side.

The backswing should happen at the same time as the first movement of a shot. Make sure you take the bat back with your arms, not just your hands, to ensure a powerful swing.

FRONT FOOT **DEFENCE**

A solid defence is the base from which all good batsmen build. Even the best players in the world cannot attack every ball. A good defence is vital throughout your innings but will be particularly useful early on as you look to play yourself in.

The forward defence is played to a good length ball pitching in line with the stumps. A good length means the ball is slightly too short to drive but not short enough to play off the back foot.

COACHING POINTS

- First move your leading shoulder and head towards the ball.

BE THE BEST

Remember to move your leading shoulder and head to the ball first. Your feet should follow automatically or else you would fall over! If your foot moves first your head will stay a long way from the ball, increasing the chances of missing or edging it. If your head is over the ball you can adjust if the ball swings, seams or spins and you can direct the ball safely down in front of you.

- Your front foot should follow your head and shoulder, to take a good stride towards the ball.
- Bend your front leg to take your body weight with your back leg straight.
- Your bat should come down straight with the face angled slightly towards the ground.
- At the point of contact your head should be over the ball with your eyes level.
- Your bat should be just forward of your front leg with no gap between bat and pad.
- You should be balanced so you are able to hold your position.

Target

To stop the ball getting you out. Look for a quick single.

Common fault

Many players push too hard at the ball when playing a defensive shot. This will make the ball go up in the air. Instead, wait for the ball

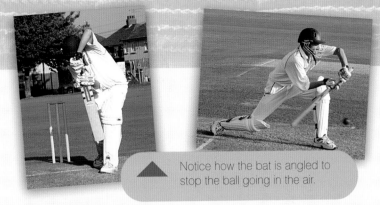

Notice how the bat is angled to stop the ball going in the air.

to hit the bat rather than pushing at it. Then the ball will drop down safely. This is known as playing with 'soft hands'.

Practice

- Start with a feeder opposite the batsman, about 6 metres away.
- The feeder delivers the ball underarm into a target zone 1–1.5 metres from the bat.
- The batsman plays a forward defence to the ball, or leaves it if it pitches outside off-stump.
- When you feel confident, move the feeder back and feed the ball overarm into the zone. As the ball is coming faster and from a higher trajectory it will be more difficult for the batsman to play.

- To make the drill harder, move the feeder back and feed overarm from on one knee.

Next step

- Introduce a wicketkeeper and a fielder on either side of the batsman about 2 metres away.
- The batsmen must now concentrate on making the ball bounce before it reaches the fielders. Play with soft hands.
- Each batsman faces 5 balls. They are awarded 1 point for a successful leave and 5 points for a good forward defence. They will lose 5 points each time they are bowled or caught.
- The winner is the player with the most points.

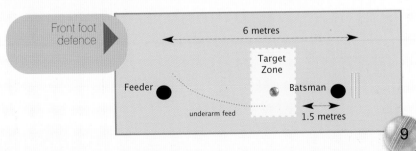

Front foot defence

6 metres

Target Zone

Feeder

Batsman

underarm feed

1.5 metres

BACK FOOT **DEFENCE**

To be a top batsman you must be able to play well off both the front and back foot. The best players in the world are equally comfortable playing off either.

The back foot defensive shot is played to a ball short of a good length that reaches the batsman around waist height. The key to playing the shot well is moving into position quickly and playing the ball with soft hands.

COACHING POINTS

• Move your back foot back and across towards off-stump, using the full depth of the crease.

1. The batsman's first move is back and across.
2. The batsman's head is in line with the ball.
3. Great use of the depth of the crease.

• Keep your back foot parallel to the crease taking the weight on your back leg.

• Move your front foot back to a balanced position.

• Make contact with the ball underneath your eyes with your head still.

• Play with a straight bat ensuring your hands are high and angle the bat down towards the ground.

• Play with soft hands; allow the ball to hit the bat rather than pushing at the ball.

Target

To stop the ball getting you out. Look for a quick single.

Common fault

Players often move their back foot back towards leg-stump rather than off-stump. This puts them at greater risk of being caught by the wicketkeeper, as they may play at balls outside off-stump they could leave. If you play a shot with your head a long way from the ball you are much more likely to edge it or miss it altogether. It is also dangerous if the ball moves towards the batsman or 'follows him'. This can leave the player cramped for room and he may hit the ball upwards or be hit on the body. By moving towards off-stump it is easier to judge the line of the ball and react to any movement it may make off the seam.

Practice

This drill focuses on using the depth of your crease, judging the length of the ball and playing with soft hands. It can be practised

with just two people but is more fun with several.

- You will need one batsman, one wicketkeeper, a feeder about 11 metres from the batsman's crease and at least one fielder on each side 4 metres from the bat.
- The feeder feeds the ball overarm into the target zone about 3 metres from the bat. The batsman must play back foot defensive with soft hands to stop fielders catching it. The batsman swaps when caught out.

Next step

Fielders can catch the batsman out after the ball has bounced once as long as they use one hand. This will really test the batsman's 'soft hands'.

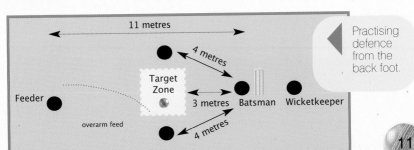

11 metres
4 metres
Target Zone
Feeder
3 metres   Batsman   Wicketkeeper
overarm feed
4 metres

Practising defence from the back foot.

11

LEAVING THE **BALL**

It may not be the most exciting shot in the world but learning how to leave well is a crucial part of a solid defence. Opening batsmen in particular must be able to judge line and length quickly and decide which balls to play at and which to leave. Making the wrong decision could cost you your wicket.

FRONT FOOT

The key is to ensure that your head is in line with off-stump, so you know that any balls pitching outside this line are likely to miss the stumps. If you are leaving a full ball you should leave on the front foot, while you should look to leave short bowling on the back foot.

Learning to leave well is important for all batsmen.

COACHING POINTS

- Try and judge line and length as early as you can, taking into account any swing, seam or spin on the ball.
- Get your head in line with the off-stump. Move your front leg forward inside the line of the delivery taking weight on your bent front leg to ensure a stable base.
- Keep your eye on the ball and leave with bat and hands close to your body. Raise your bat and hands higher than the ball ensuring bat and gloves are out of the way.

- Keep your head level and remain balanced throughout. Don't fall to the off-side.

BACK FOOT

Good players must be happy to leave both full and short length deliveries. In Test matches batsmans are often bombarded with quick, short-pitched bowling. When leaving short-pitched bowling, batsmans know that the ball is usually going to miss the stumps as it is too high, yet they have to get their own bodies out of the way to ensure they do not hit the ball in the air or get struck on the body.

There are two ways to leave the short ball effectively:

- **Ducking:** This is where the batsman ducks underneath the ball. Remember to keep your eyes on the ball at all times.
- **Swaying:** When swaying out of the way of the ball, drop your hands below the ball, stay side on and keep looking at the ball.

Target

To leave the ball safely, keeping bat and gloves out of the way of the ball.

Ducking is one way of taking evasive action.

A good example of swaying out of the way.

FRONT FOOT **DRIVING**

The drive is one of the most exciting and stylish shots in the game. England captain Michael Vaughan is one of the best drivers in cricket. His ability to get in position early and time the ball sweetly makes him a great example to watch.

There are three types of front foot drive; the off-drive (also known as the cover drive), straight drive and on-drive. The names of the shots refer to the area of the field to which you are hitting the ball.

For example the off-drive is played through the off-side, towards cover. The straight drive is played straight down the ground and the on-drive is hit through the on-side towards mid-on.

A drive is usually played to a full-length ball known as a half-volley. This is slightly fuller than the good length that would normally demand a forward defensive shot.

THE STRAIGHT DRIVE

The straight drive is played to a half-volley pitching from middle-stump to just outside off. The key difference between the straight drive and forward defensive shot is that, rather

than waiting for the ball to hit the bat, the batsman should hit the ball with a full swing of the bat. Though this is an attacking shot that can be struck powerfully, it is important to keep your head over the ball and keep the ball on the ground.

Coaching points

- First move your leading shoulder and head towards the ball.

- Your front foot should follow the movement of your head and shoulder so you take a good stride towards the ball.

- Take a full backswing to ensure you can hit the ball powerfully.

- At the point of contact your head should be over the ball with your front knee slightly bent to take your weight.

- Your bat should come down in a straight line and hit the ball with the full face of the bat.

- After contact you should follow

through with your bat over your leading shoulder (full drive) or hands level with your eyes (check drive).

- You should be balanced and able to hold your position.

GO FOR IT!

Keep your head and leading shoulder in line with where you want the ball to go for as long as possible.

Target

To hit the ball along the ground for four between mid-on and mid-off.

Common fault

Young players often hit their straight drives on the leg-side. Usually this is because the bottom hand is in control of the shot. Make sure you are not gripping the bat too hard with your bottom hand. The top hand should control your front foot shots.

THE OFF-DRIVE

The off-drive shares many similarities with the straight drive and the coaching points above also apply to this shot. The key difference is that

▲ Notice how head, hands and feet stay in line throughout the shot.

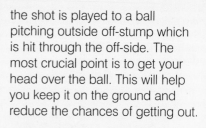

BE THE BEST

Keep your head over the ball as long as possible, and carry on looking down at the point of contact even after you have hit it. This will help you keep a good body position and hit the ball along the ground.

the shot is played to a ball pitching outside off-stump which is hit through the off-side. The most crucial point is to get your head over the ball. This will help you keep it on the ground and reduce the chances of getting out.

COACHING POINTS

The coaching points for the off-drive are similar to those for the straight drive. The key thing to remember is to point your head and leading shoulder towards the line of the ball and maintain this shape. If the ball is to travel towards the off-side your shoulders must stay pointing in this direction throughout the shot.

Target

To hit the ball along the ground for four between cover and mid-off.

Common fault

Players often try to hit the ball too hard and end up leaning back when they play the shot. This leads to them hitting the

 To strike the ball powerfully remember to follow through with the bat over your leading shoulder.

16

ball in the air, or even
missing it.

THE ON-DRIVE

This is one of the hardest shots
to play in cricket. The key to the
shot is to maintain good balance
throughout. The on-drive is
played to a ball which pitches
around middle and leg to leg-
stump, and it should be hit
between mid-wicket and mid-on.
Some young players try to hit the
ball too square, which is risky as it
often involves playing with a
closed bat face. This means you
are more likely to miss the ball and
risk being out LBW. The straighter
you look to hit the on-drive the less
risky it is and the more chance
there is of scoring runs.

Coaching points

Most of the coaching points for the
on-drive are the same as those for
the straight and cover drives,
though there are a few crucial
differences. It is important to
remember to keep your head and
shoulders in line with the ball
throughout the shot. It is also
crucial to create a solid base. When
playing the on-drive the stride
length is normally shorter than for
the other drives. It is also useful to
keep your front leg on the leg-side
of the ball as this allows you to

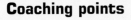 The on-drive requires a
shorter stride than the
other drives to help
maintain balance. Make
sure your head does not
fall away to the off-side at
the point of contact.

BE THE BEST

Keep your head over your
leading shoulder to help
you stay balanced
throughout the shot.

bring the bat through straight and hit with the full bat face. It is important to ensure that there is no gap between bat and pad when playing the shot.

Target

To hit the ball for four along the ground between mid-wicket and mid-on.

Practice

This drill can be done in small groups or on your own. If you are in a group, place fielders in the goal to act as 'goalkeepers' and field the ball.

- Place a ball on a tee (if you do not have a tee, use a plastic cup). Set up a 'goal' with a width of 4–5 metres a minimum of 11 metres from the ball.

- The batsman takes his/her stance a little back from the ball so he/she has to step towards it to play the drive.

- Attempt to strike the ball along the ground and into the goal. Have a few goes and then swap with your team mates.

- You can change the drill by moving the goals to practise your cover and on-drives.

Next step

Next, have someone feed the ball, as it is harder to hit a moving ball than a stationary one.

- The feeder stands 11 metres away and provides the batsman with an underarm bobble feed. This means the ball should bounce several times before reaching the batsmen.

- This type of feed means the batsman should always get a half-volley to hit. Step 3 is a feed bouncing only once.

- Continue with the same set-up using goals and fielders as before.

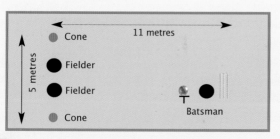

Always make sure fielders are a safe distance from the batsman to avoid injury.

England opener Alistair Cook drives for four through the off-side.

MOVING OUT OF THE CREASE TO DRIVE

You will often see top batsmen advancing outside of their crease to attack spinners and some medium pace bowlers. This is done to create scoring opportunities and put the bowler off his natural line and length. It is particularly useful against spinners as batsmen can get to the ball before it has had a chance to spin. The aim of coming out of the crease is to attack the bowler though good players are able to adjust and play defensively if the ball isn't right to attack. Here are some important points to bear in mind when attempting to come down the wicket.

- **Don't come down the wicket too early:** If you start advancing before the bowler has released the ball he will be able to adjust his delivery, which could lead to a stumping. Leave it as late as possible.

- **Lead with your head and shoulder:** This will ensure that you are balanced and are in the perfect position to attack.

- **Take a big first stride:** This will help you gain momentum and get a good distance outside

There are two methods of moving your feet to come down the wicket (see footwork, on page 21).

your crease. If you are to change the length of the bowler's delivery you will have to get well down the pitch.

- **Keep your head and eyes steady:** If your head falls to one side you will lose balance, which will make you mistime your shot or miss the ball completely.

- **Use smooth footwork:** There are two ways in which batsmen use their feet when coming down the wicket. One method is to move your back foot behind your front foot (see pic 1). The second method is to bring your back foot up to your front like a side step (see pic 2). Try both methods and work out which one is best for you.

THE LOFTED DRIVE

The lofted drive often goes hand in hand with using your feet and is used to attack bowlers. A batsman uses this shot to intentionally hit the ball in the air. Some of the coaching points are the same as for the normal drive shots though there a few important differences.

COACHING POINTS

- Move your front foot towards the line of the ball with your head

and leading shoulder slightly behind.

- Take a big backswing and bring the bat through straight towards the line of the ball.

- Play the ball earlier than you would for a conventional drive.

- As you hit the ball your head and eyes should be still, with your body weight just behind the point of contact.

- Follow through with your bat finishing right up over your leading shoulder.

Target

To hit the ball for four or six straight down the ground.

Common fault

Many players look up to see where the ball has gone before completing the shot. This causes them to lean back with their head in the air. As a result they mistime the ball.

BACK FOOT **DRIVING**

The back foot drive is played to a ball pitching short of a length and bouncing about thigh height. A ball pitching short of a length is fuller than one you might cut, or pull, but is too short to play on the front foot. It is played with a straight bat and, as with other backfoot shots, balance and use of the crease are the key. The emphasis of this shot is on timing rather than trying to hit the ball too hard. Though it is a difficult shot to master, it can be a safe way of scoring runs off the back foot as you are using the full face and length of the bat. This makes it easier to adjust to a delivery that may move late or bounce unexpectedly.

COACHING POINTS

- Move your back foot back and towards the line of the ball using the depth of the crease.
- Keep your back foot parallel to the crease and bring your front foot to a balanced position (see pic 1, opposite).
- Keep your head still and upright. Try to stay as tall as you can with your weight on the back foot.

- Use a short backswing and attempt to 'punch' the ball with a straight bat, making contact underneath your eyes.
- Make sure your hands are above the ball and you have a high front elbow to keep the ball down.
- Finish with your hands up in line with your eyes in a checked follow-through (see pic 2, opposite).

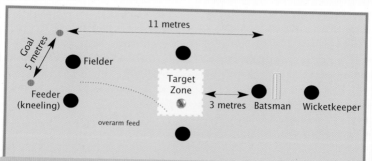

Basic practice for the back foot drive. You can experiment by moving the goal.

Target

To stay on top of the ball and hit it for four through the off-side.

Practice

- Set this up as you did for the front foot driving drill with a 'goal' 11 metres away about 4–5 metres in width and a target area about 3 metres in front of the batsman.

- A feeder kneels opposite the batsman and feeds the ball overarm aiming for the target.

- The batsman must play a backfoot drive, looking to hit the ball back through the goal. You can move the goal to practise hitting the ball in different areas and vary its width to make it more difficult.

- You can introduce scoring to make the drill more competitive.

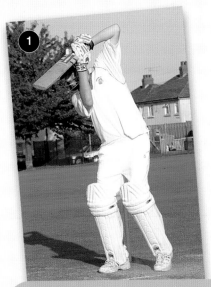

 Use a checked follow-through to stay in control of the shot.

THE SQUARE CUT

The cut shot is an explosive stroke used to punish short deliveries wide of off-stump. Good cutters of the ball get into position quickly and use controlled power to execute the shot well. A good shot is hit powerfully down into the ground through the cover point area with a horizontal bat.

There are several types of cut shot. The upper cut is a riskier version of the square cut where batsmen aim to hit the ball in the air over the in-field.

Another variation is the late cut, which is usually played to spinners. The batsman plays the ball as late as possible and delicately clips it behind square relying on the natural pace of the ball to do the work.

The best way to learn how to play the variations of the cut shot is to first master the square cut.

COACHING POINTS

- Move your feet back and towards the line of the ball.
- Keep your back foot parallel to the crease line and use the full depth of the crease.
- Take your weight on the back foot and keep your head over the ball and your eyes level.
- Take a big backswing, ensuring you get your hands higher than the ball.
- Hit the ball with a horizontal bat.
- Hit down into the ball, making sure the ball is played into the ground.
- Continue your follow-through up over your left shoulder.

Target

To hit the ball for four square on the off side.

Common fault

Make sure you hit the ball using your arms rather than just your wrist and hands. If you cut with your wrist and hands you will have less power and control over the shot.

Practice

Place a goal about 10 metres from the batsman square of the wicket

Hit the ball with arms extended for maximum power and control.

on the off-side. The goal should be 3–4 metres wide with one or two fielders guarding it. A feeder kneels about 3 metres in front of the batsman and feeds the ball underarm as a full toss just above stump height outside the batsman's off-stump. Try to score in the goal as often as you can.

Next step

Once you are confident with a full toss feed, attempt to cut a bouncing ball. The feeder moves further back and throws overarm at a target about 3 metres in front of the batsman and a little way outside off-stump. This makes the drill more difficult as the batsman must judge the way that the ball is going to bounce.

Use a full follow-through over your shoulder.

THE **PULL**

The pull shot can be one of the most spectacular in cricket. It is an attacking shot played to a short ball too straight to cut.

Good batsmen can play the pull shot to balls just outside off-stump and those pitching on the stumps, but while you are learning the shot it is best to play it to balls pitching on or just outside leg-stump. Like the cut shot it is all about controlled aggression and quick footwork. Players such as Ponting and Pietersen get into position so quickly that they can turn a ball that is barely short into an easy boundary. It is crucial to hit down into the ball and keep your head in a balanced position.

COACHING POINTS

- Move your back foot back and across towards off-stump, keeping it parallel with the batting crease.
- Take a big backswing, ensuring your hands are higher than the ball.
- Bring your front foot back and towards the left side so you are chest-on to the ball.
- Keeping your head still, hit down into the ball with a horizontal bat.

Get in position early and hit down on the ball.

Hitting the ball off a tee is a good way to practise when first learning the pull shot. This picture shows a left-handed batsman.

- Transfer your body weight from the back leg to the front leg.
- Follow through with your bat finishing over your front shoulder.
- Finish in a balanced position.

Top players use a variation called the pivot pull against fast bowling, but you should first attempt to master the version described here. It is most effective against spin and medium pace.

Target

To hit the ball for four between square leg and mid-wicket.

Common fault

Remember to keep your head still and over the ball when you play the shot. Many players try to hit the ball too hard and end up leaning back as they strike it. This sends the ball in the air, increasing the risk of being caught.

Practice

Place a tee on top of a stump 30–50 centimetres outside the batting crease in line with middle and leg-stump. Place a goal square on the leg-side 15 metres from the batsman. The batsman strikes the ball off the tee and through the goal. Make the goal smaller and add points to make the drill harder.

Next step

Remove the stump and tee. Bring in a feeder 11 metres away to throw the ball overarm at a target 3 metres from the batsman. The batsman must now take into account the bounce of the ball and the slight variations in line that occur with a feeder, which will make the practice more difficult.

THE LEG **GLANCE**

The leg glance is one of the more elegant shots in cricket. It is played to a full-length ball just outside leg-stump. The shot uses the pace of the ball to direct it behind square on the leg-side.

England's Alistair Cook plays this shot well. He watches the ball right on to the bat before slightly closing the face to angle the ball away. It is important to maintain good balance and to close the bat face as late as possible. It requires good timing rather than power.

COACHING POINTS

• Move your head and front shoulder towards the line of the ball.

• Move your front foot towards the line of the ball, creating a strong base.

• Bring the bat through straight with your top hand in control.

• Use your wrists to close the bat face at the point of contact.

• At the point of contact, your head should be still and in line with the ball.

• Avoid pushing at the ball; allow it to come on to the bat.

Target

To hit the ball for runs behind square on the leg side.

Common fault

Some players let their head fall towards the off-side when they play this shot and finish off

Keep your head up to stay in a balanced position.

Australia's Ricky Ponting plays the leg glance to good effect in a one-day international against England.

balance. As a result they risk hitting the ball into the air.

Practice

This shot is best practised with pace on the ball. To start off you may want a feeder to deliver underarm full tosses aimed at leg-stump but the best practice is with a full overarm feed. The feeder should stand 11 metres away and aim for a target about 1 metre from the bat in line with leg-stump.

BE THE BEST

The leg glance involves timing rather than power. Allow the ball to run off the bat face rather than pushing hard at the ball.

THE SWEEP **SHOT**

The sweep shot, though difficult to play, is a useful weapon against spin bowling. It is played to a good length ball pitching from just outside off-stump to outside leg, but while you are learning stick to balls outside leg-stump. The sweep is the only front foot shot to be played using a horizontal bat and requires excellent judgment of length and spin.

COACHING POINTS

- Take a long stride forward, towards the line of the ball, with your front leg and lower your back leg to the ground.
- Take a large backswing, ensuring your hands are higher than the ball.
- Extend your arms to hit the ball out in front of you keeping your head still over your front knee.
- Hit down into the ball, with a horizontal bat, square on the leg-side.
- At the point of contact ensure your head is still and your body remains balanced and upright.
- Continue your follow-through up over your leading shoulder.

Target

To hit the ball along the ground for runs behind square on the leg side.

Common fault

Many players move their head towards the off-side when playing this shot. This can cause them to miss the ball or hit it in the air. Keep your head perfectly still and you should make good contact.

Variations

There are several variations of the sweep shot, for example:

- **The slog sweep:** This involves the same initial movements as the sweep. However, players will aim to hit the ball in the air over the in-field. This is done by taking the bat from a low to a high position, hitting up through the ball.
- **The reverse sweep:** This is a very complex shot to play and

few players even attempt it. The technique is very similar to the sweep but the batsman reverses the face of their bat and so hits the ball square, or behind square, on the off-side.

Practice

You can start off practising the sweep shot by hitting off a cone, or by using a 'drop feed'.
- A feeder stands in front of the batsman, far enough away to avoid being hit by the bat.
- The feeder holds the ball at arm's length in front of him and, when the batsman says 'drop' simply drops the ball directly down.
- Let the ball bounce 2 or 3 times before playing the sweep.

Next step

When the batsman feels confident hitting the sweep shot from a drop feed, move on to an underarm feed.
- The feeder throws the ball underarm so that it bounces about 2–3 metres away from the batsman.
- Practise feeding the ball on different lines and setting up goals in different areas of the leg-side to replicate a match situation.

Take a big stride towards the ball and hit with both arms fully extended to control the shot.

Great batting is not just about hitting the ball. Running well between the wickets can be the difference between winning and losing. The key is communication and awareness.

COMMUNICATION

Keep the calling simple: YES if you want to run, NO if you don't and WAIT if you're not sure, quickly followed by yes or no. Talk to your batting partner between overs. You should discuss gaps in the field and which fielders are slower or have weaker throwing arms. If you see a throw coming, tell your partner which end it is going to.

BACKING UP

Always be on the lookout for a chance to run. If you are the non-striker, this means backing up. Walk towards the striker as the bowler runs in, keeping part of your bat behind the line until the bowler has bowled. Carry on down the pitch until your partner has played a shot. You should finish backing up at least 2 metres from your crease. Be ready to run or return to your end quickly.

MAKING YOUR GROUND

When trying to make your ground, stretch out your arm at full length. This can gain a few crucial centimetres and mean the difference between being in or out.

TURNING

When turning for a second or third run, always turn towards the part of the field where the ball is. This may mean changing which hand you hold the bat in. When running a two with the ball on the off-side, the striker should turn with the bat in his left hand so that he can see if it is safe to run.

Running well between the wickets can be the difference between winning and losing.